SMART MONEY CONCEPT

I0505272

Market Structure, Supply and Demand, Order Block, Mastering The Market

Harold Keith

TABLE OF CONTENT

INTROUDTION

Capital that institutional monetary help, public banks, and different prepared experts or money related foundations control.Overseen by master monetary supporters can expect market models and make a huge piece of the advantages. marvelous cash believed was at beginning a wagering term, where it proposes the players that have wide data on the activity that they bet on or have insider information that the standard public can't get to.In this model, you will figure out a workable method for exchanging wise money normal market, how to utilize different time frame evaluation to fine section and leave focuses, some new strategy in forex with SMC, Likewise the cost development pointers.

The guide will assist with understanding and anticipate the following development and it will cause you to comprehend where you are, whether are you in adjustment or Continuation. Presently, we will talk about the market structure. Market Construction for the most part concludes who is in charge since we need to bring passage into the controlling side. Smart money strategy essentially the foundation of two things market construction and liquidity

This is strategy that will help you understand about the total picture of market based on market structure,supply and demand,order block.

CHAPTER ONE

SMART MONEY TRADING IN SUPPLY AND DEMAND ZONES

Smart money trader a ton the forex market. They use market pay to move the expense. The stock zone is the region or a zone where huge sell orders from the keen money happen achieving an imbalance among market pay, where the stock is a higher need than demand which makes the expense of the cash fall. Where, demand zone is the region or a zone where gigantic orders of acquisition from the shocking money occur, which achieves an inconsistency where deals is more certain than supply, which rises the expense of the money

STRUCTURE OF MARKET

The cost goes through the going with stages

1. AGGREGATION
2. REACCUMULATION
3. UPTREND
4. DISSEMINATION
5. REARRANGEMENT
6. DOWNTREN

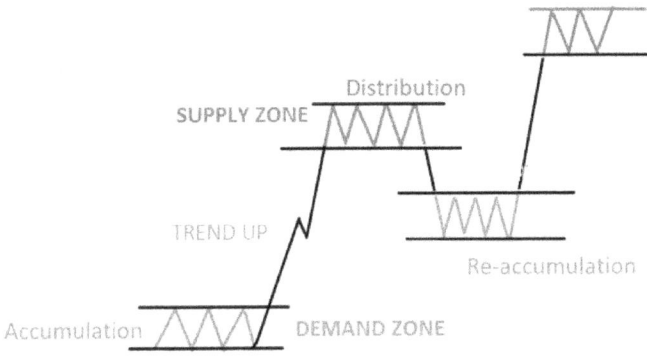

ACCUMULATION smart money is taken out the drifting load of stock by purchasing, this affiliation is called aggregating

Design UP splendid money firmly moving costs up

Assignment SM will exploit the more conspicuous costs got in the social occasion to take benefits by starting to offer the stock back to the befuddled agents/financial allies

Laws of supply and demand trading

All monetary business regions work on the general law of Market income.

Law of Interest The higher the cost of a thing, the less the interest (purchasers would rather not buy at a more inordinate cost) and the lower the value, the higher the interest (purchasers need to purchase at a negligible cost)

The Law of Supply-the higher the value, the higher the stock (transporters need to sell at a more beyond ludicrous cost) and lower the cost, cut down the supply(sellers would rather not supply at a lower cost

What are supply and demand Zones

Could we investigate Cunning 50 STOCK

Supply-demand is just the limit of what can help or hinder

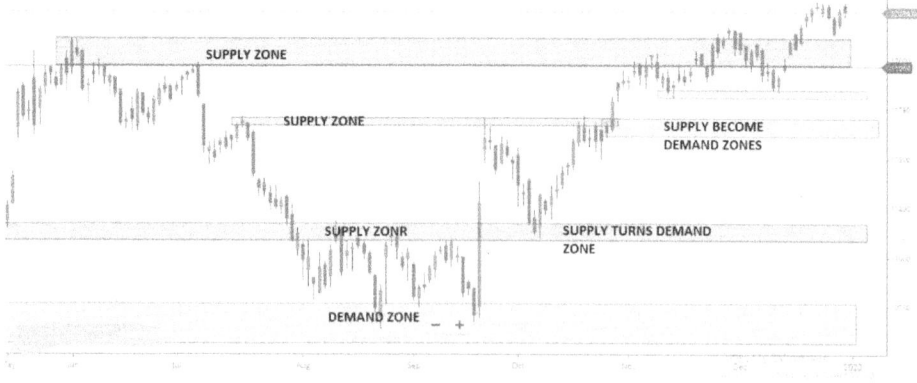

In the structure above you can see an interest zone (sweeping assistance level)

what's more, a store zone (wide area of opposition).

What we need to find at the cost zones where supply overpowers sales and where requesting overpowers supply.

- The past is known as SUPPLY ZONES. Precisely whenever the market chances upon SUPPLY ZONES, the cost will drop. Then, at that point, you can get cash by shorting the market.
- The last decision is market Requesting ZONE. With the backing of interest, the cost will rise. Then, you can help in a long position.
- On the off chance that the stock zone is broken it changes into an interest zone, pullback test from the interest zone you can go long

The best technique to Find organic market Zones in Trading Two phases to recognize the natural market zones

- Take a gander at the design and try to see moderate huge moderate candles. Cost should moves a remarkable plan
- Spread out the base (regularly sideways cost activity area) from which cost began the catalyst move

Different Kinds of Natural market Game plans

There are different regular market zone plans. A piece of the more prominent ones are displayed under:

Design Incessant BASE
- ☐RALLY BASE RALLY(RBR)
- ☐DOWN BASE DOWN (DBD)

Design Reversal BASE
- ☐RALLY BASE DROP (RBD)
- ☐DOWN BASE meeting (DBR)

Besides,

FLIP ZONE

TREND CONTINOUS BASE

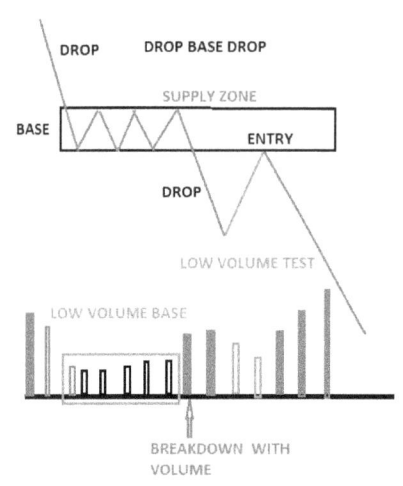

DROP   DROP BASE DROP

SUPPLY ZONE

BASE

ENTRY

DROP

LOW VOLUME TEST

LOW VOLUME BASE

BREAKDOWN WITH VOLUME

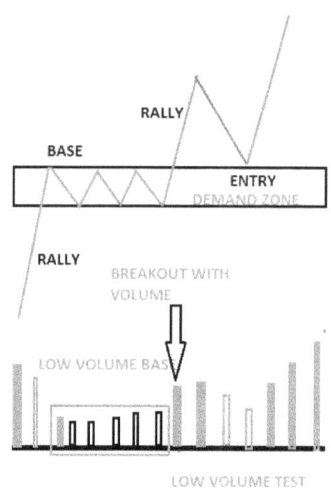

RALLY

BASE

ENTRY

DEMAND ZONE

RALLY

BREAKOUT WITH VOLUME

LOW VOLUME BASE

LOW VOLUME TEST

TREND REVERSAL BASE

RALLY BASED ROP

SUPPLY ZONE

BASE

ENTRY

DROP

RALLY

DOWN BASE RALLY

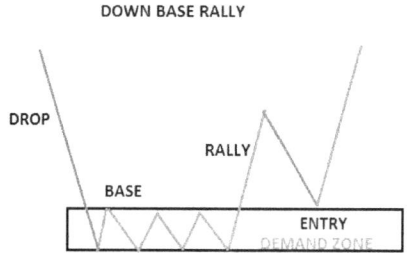

DROP

RALLY

BASE

ENTRY

DEMAND ZONE

FLIP ZONE

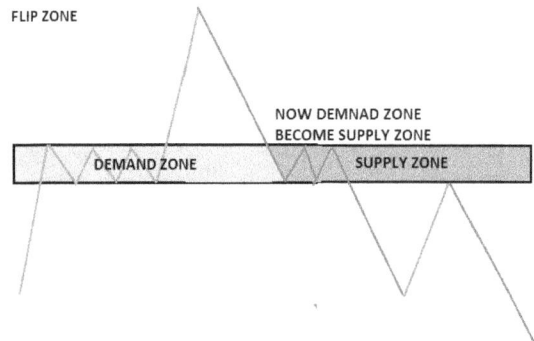

NOW DEMNAD ZONE
BECOME SUPPLY ZONE

DEMAND ZONE   SUPPLY ZONE

STRENGTH OF Market revenue ZONE

How did the cost leave the level, STRENGTH OF THE MOVE

The Thinking: The more grounded the cost makes some partition from a zone, the more out-of-balance market income are at that zone. A significant requesting is set by watchful cash

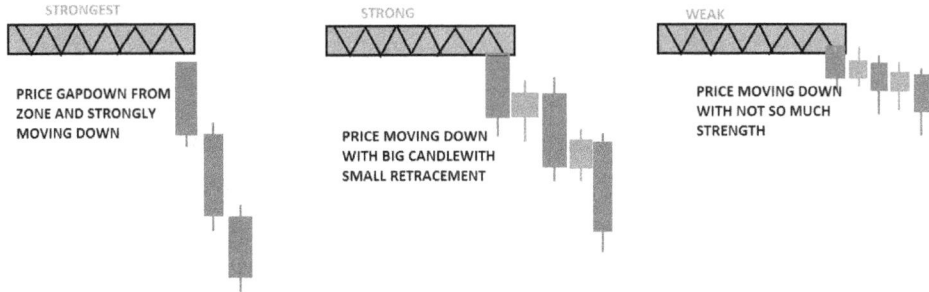

How long did the expense spend at the zone, TIME AT LEVEL

The Thinking: The less time cost spends at a zone, the more out-of-balance normal market are at the cost level. Shrewd cash firmly entering

At cost levels with normal market zone more out of equilibrium, the cost will contribute immaterial extent of energy at the level

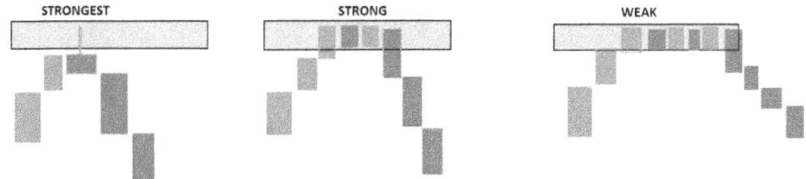

The less time price spends at a level, THE STRONGER THE LEVEL

Once more how far did the cost make a division from the zone going before getting to the zone?

The Thinking: The farther cost makes a division from a zone prior to getting back to that zone, the more recognizable the compensation to plausibility and likelihood.

Precisely when the cost returns to that supply level for our short section, we have an insightful thought about where the purchasers are (the interest) and correspondingly as essentially, where they are not.

How frequently is the expense pushing toward the zone?

Freshness OF BASE

First-time stock backtrack to the base is the most grounded to enter

When does Supply/Solicitation break

After a zone is endeavored for the most part or during a solid move, Market income levels finally break. Because of the additional orders being set off and step by

step cleared out, or a dazzling extent of requesting the other way breaking the level.

Price action

- Expecting that the cost stays close by at these zones and doesn't fall a lot of then there is a high likelihood that they will break the zone
- A solid move to the zone could break the zone
- low volume test affirm the zone

HOW TO ENTER Solicitation AND SUPPLY Using Worth Action

1.Find SD zone on HTF(HIGHER Timeframe) then, accept that the cost will appear at this level

2.See any assertion or dismissal from this zone on exchanging time frame(TTF)

3.Any inversion cost development signal on TTF

4.Passage toward the overall plan

Expect setting downtrend, regard rally to the stock zone on TTF, then, at that point, any deplorable inversion Father signal for a segment short

Besides, notice the volume on these inversions. A low volume test is a decent sign and they are unimaginably possible exchanges.

TIPS for day exchanging earlier day high and earlier day low is the normal market zone. look cost activity around there for confirmation or dismissal of these zones

We ought to do a model

Find the normal market zone in a higher time span

In an hourly timeframe we track down the zone

raised viewpoint shows

1. whether plan up or down - figures out which side we ought to be on

2. Where are the raised point of view backing and sales levels?

We would rather not long under the stock zone

Precisely when THE Value Techniques Requesting ZONE

WE Acknowledge that Should SEE Indication OF Courage Worth Activity FOR

Demand OF THE ZONE

1 Power LOSS(DECREASING Light Reach AND BODY

2.LOWER WICK

3.Blend OF BOTH RED AND GREEN Fire

Section on the exchanging time span

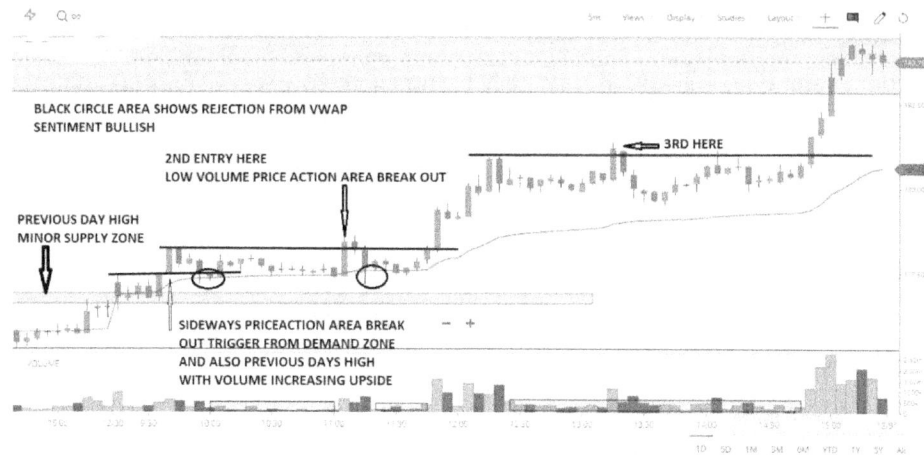

Section SIGNAL Light

Candles AT Normal market

- ☐☐PIN BAR
- ☐☐Dousing
- ☐☐OUTSIDE Fire

Chances Enhancers model

1.Exchange with the model

2.On the distant chance that Record AND Locale SHOWS POSITIVE, GO
LONG FROM Interest ZONE

CHAPTER TWO

HOW TO TRADE WITH SMART MONEY

There are three essential signs of brilliant cash activity which we can distinguish with Worth Movement and volume and can trade with them

- Sideways Worth Movement District
- ☐Intense Initiation Development
- ☐Strong Excusal (of Successive Expenses)
- ☐Sideways Worth Movement District

Sideways cost activity region

Look for sideways cost activity region. Those are very basic spots since Splendid Money is gathering its circumstances there. Constantly watch for such locales, paying little heed to which time frame you use. FOR continuation of an ongoing example these sideways cost movement locales should be low volume

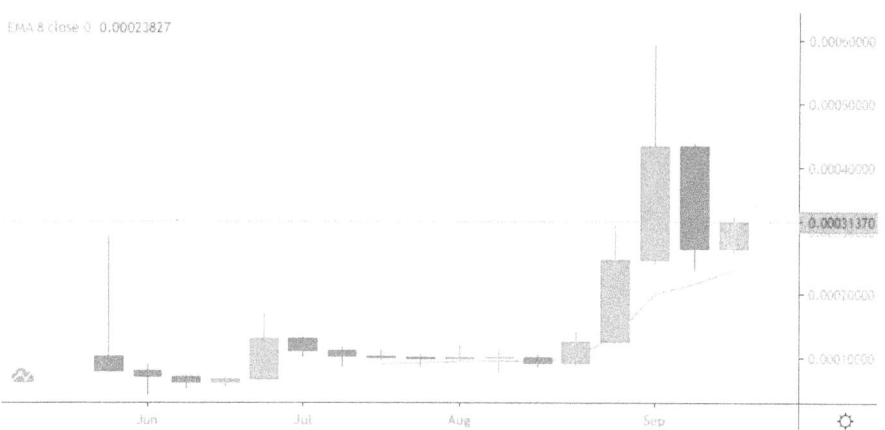

Forceful Inception Movement

Forceful action is basically a basic expense improvement. It is achieved by intense buyers(SM) pushing the expense higher or by powerful sellers(SM) who are pushing the expense lower. This sort of strong exchanging regularly occurs later sideways cost action development. What happens is that Splendid Money is fostering its circumstances (in sideways locales), and when they are done with that, they start powerful exchanging to control and push the expense toward any way they need. This is how they get cash. They foster their positions bit by bit and subtle, and a short time later they start an example to make those positions useful.

Right when the expense is moving in a fast example, there isn't much of chance to put any more gigantic positions. Thus, Insightful Money needs to hoard its circumstances before the move. Coming up next is an outline of sideways cost action districts followed by strong origin development:

Strong Excusal (of sequential costs)

Strong excusal infers unforeseen expense reversal from either successive expense levels. This model is made when the expense goes one way powerfully and subsequently turns quickly and with a comparable aggression and speed goes the substitute way. A model would be a sort of fire called the pin bar. Anyway, the pin bar isn't the vitally visual sort serious solid areas for of. There are various ways a strong excusable can appear to be. A commonplace sign of all strong excusable is antagonism and surprising reversal (2 bar reversal) What happens is that one side of the market (for example buyers) is strong and moves the expense in one way. Then, it clashes with the contrary side (for example strong purchasers) which out of the blue ends up being considerably more grounded and, shockingly, more intense. So the expense turns quickly, and the more grounded side overwhelms. The district where the contrary side took over is extraordinarily basic considering the way that it means significant solid areas for where individuals excused strongly the continuous methodology and started serious solid areas for a. Yet again this spot is colossal, taking everything into account considering the way that it will without a doubt be safeguarded later on expecting the expense draws near. It transforms into another assistance/resistance zone.

The following are a couple of examples solid areas for of:

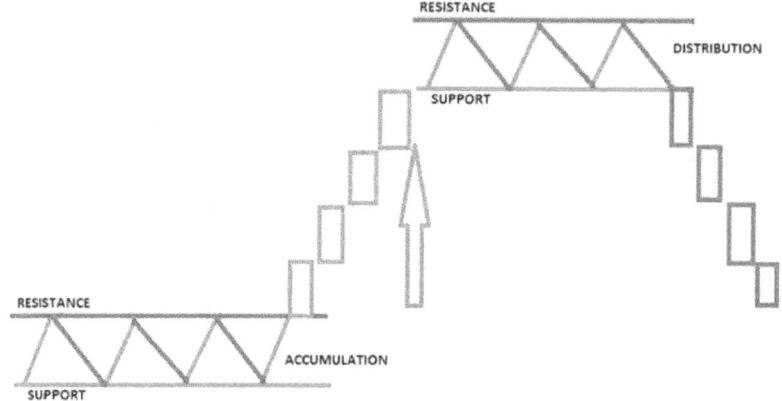

Keep in mind, where cost out of nowhere turned and headed in a different path are extremely huge. We ought to constantly keep an eye out for them in our cost activity examination

- Odd enhancer for exchanging
- Exchanging with the pattern
- Exchanging from market interest or backing obstruction level
- Exchanging with the prevailing strain

TASK

Open the graph tracks down these three Savvy Cash exercises and examines the way of behaving. This methodology deals with all time periods for example from informal investor to swing dealer

CHAPTER THREE

Smart Money Market Structure Trading using Order Block

When a large trader or institution takes a large position in a particular asset or market, its activities can essentially affect the market interest elements, prompting shifts in cost and market course. For instance, on the off chance that an enormous institutional financial backer chooses to purchase a critical number of offers in a specific organization, this can prompt expanded interest for the offers, driving up the cost. Likewise, in the event that a huge dealer takes a short situation in a specific market, this can prompt a decline popular and drive the cost down. Same as we examine patterns.

1. Uptrend Demand in Control
2. Downtrend Supply in Control

3 Things we look at before Entering are:

Step 1: Identify the Trend of Market

The first step in creating a trading strategy based on order block is to identify the market trend you want to trade. Take a gander at the general market structure (Record setting paces all around or Worse high points and Worse low points. Negative or Bullish). Market structure offers us inclination for exchanging chances. In the positively trending market, we generally hope to purchase

Step 2: Identify Key order block Zones

Once you have identified the market trend, the next step is to identify key bullish or bearish order block zones. These zones are areas where there is a significant imbalance between supply and demand. Search for bullish or negative request blocks as per the higher time span pattern. In this way, in the event that the higher time period pattern is a downtrend, you would search for a negative request block and on the off chance that you are in a bullish market, you would bullish request block

Step 3: Entry and Trade Management

Look at the lower time frames and look for the lower time frame confirmations

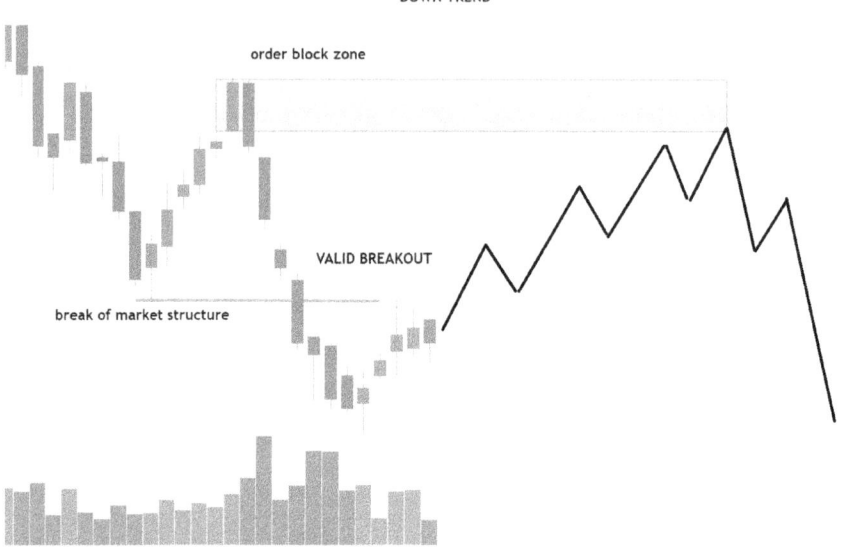

As you can see the market is in a downtrend making a lower low and lower high. Substantial negative request hindered framed. Hang tight for any negative guard at the OB zone. OW really take a look at beneath the refreshed diagram.

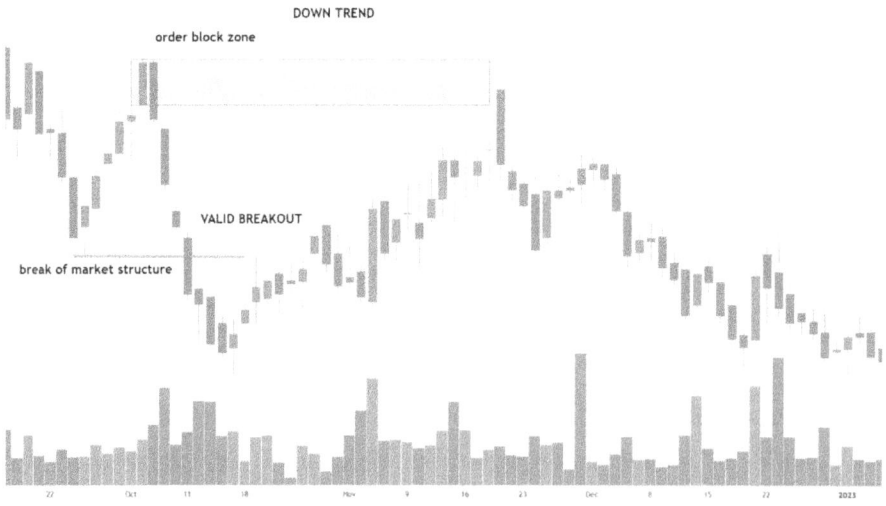

Outline till now

- Market structure who is in charge

- Order Block (area of entry)

Prior to beginning first clear a few essential parts of trends or market structure

Standards of Smart money Market structure Order Block trading

Price moves inside a primary of support and resistance. A breakout of the structural of support or resistance will lead to price movement in the next area of the support or resistance.

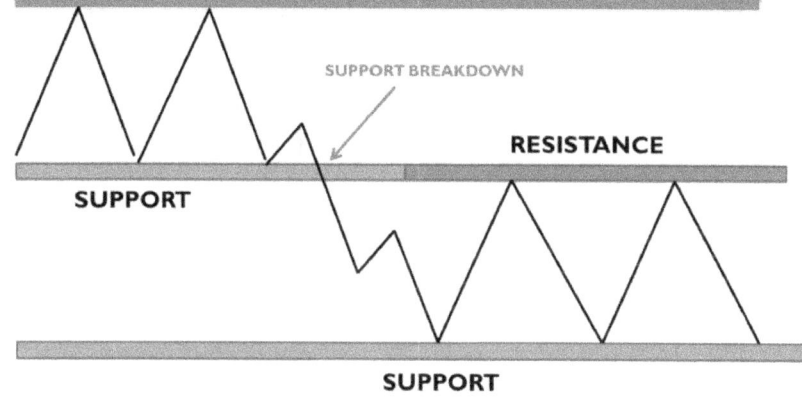

Price moves within a structural of support and resistance.
A breakout of the structural of support or resistance will lead to price movement in the next area of the support or resistance

Solid Low (SL)

At the point when the cost broke market structure was high. the depressed spot turns into major areas of strength for a. Solid Low is The Low that caused Control and Break Construction (opposition).

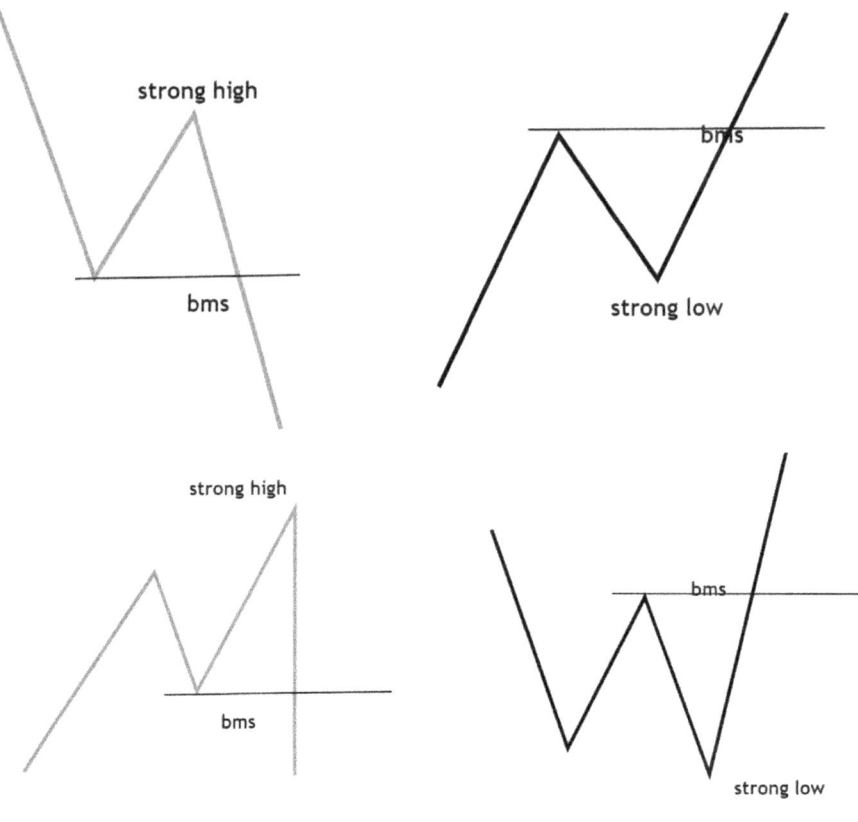

Weak High or Low

New high in an upswing and new low in a downtrend. Frail Low/High is the Low that neglects To Break Design (Feeble HIGH OR LOW Delivered Consistently FROM major areas of strength for an or Low).

- For every strong LOW, there is a weak High
- For every strong High, there is a weak Low

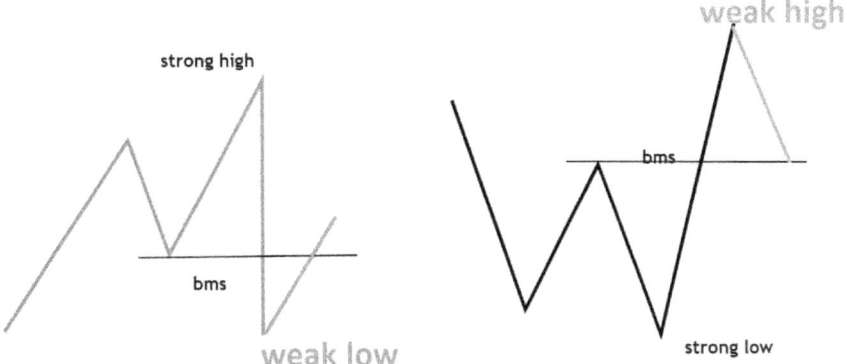

When Does Supply/Demand Break?

After a zone is tried commonly or during a solid move, Supply and Demand levels in the long run break. Because of the excess orders being set off and steadily eliminated, or a mind-boggling number of requests the other way breaking the level

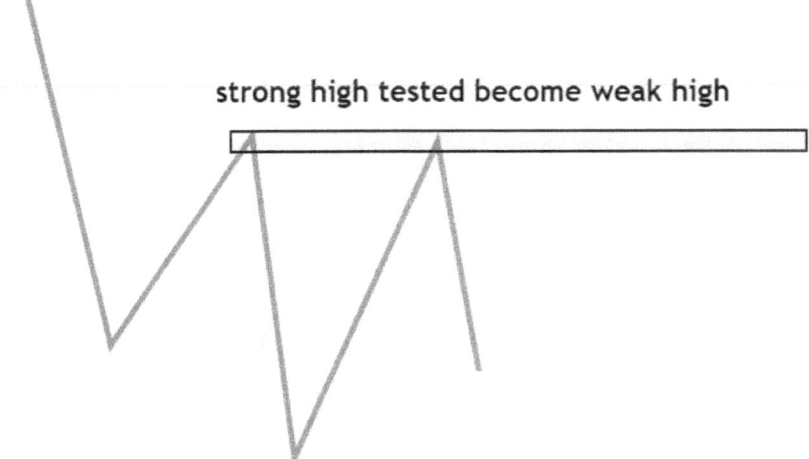

Different Types of Smart Money Market Structures in Order Block Trading Method

Periods of Market structure

The price goes through 4 Stages

1. Aggregation
2. Upswing

3. Dissemination

4. DOWNTREND

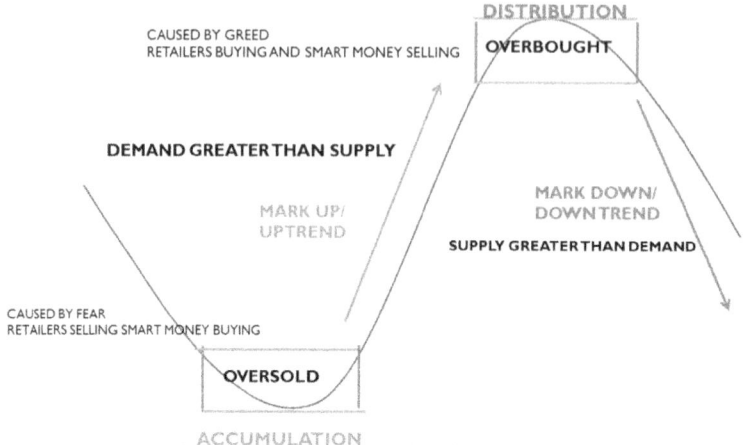

In view of the Stages 3 entry structure

- Break of market structure in upswing or downtrend

- Supply-request flip or change of character in a pattern inversion

Upswing and Down Pattern

Pattern offers us inclination for exchanging chances. In the positively trending market, we generally hope to purchase plunges

Break of Market Structure

On any Time period, when we see a break and close of a light past the design (swing high in an upswing and swing low in a downtrend) this is known as a break of construction, exceptionally basic we have broken the old construction and made another design. Break of the design framed in a pattern continuation.

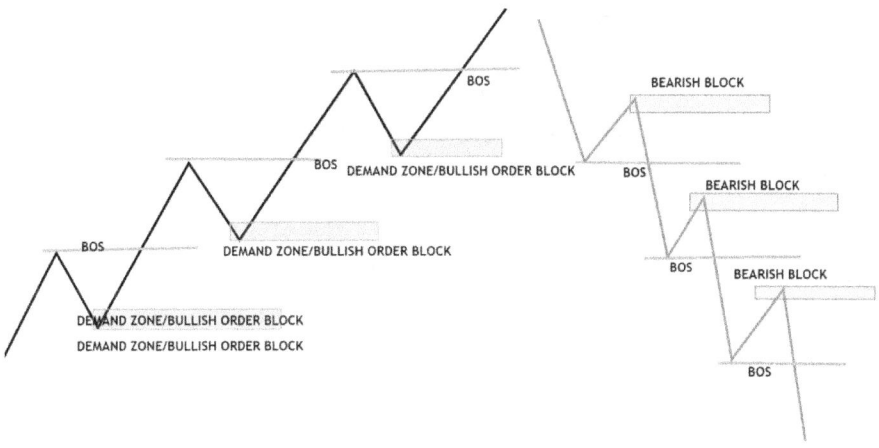

Here are the fundamental stages for carrying out the Consistent Request Block Section Strategy

Step 1: Identify the Market Structure and wait for the break of the market structure

The first step is to identify the market structure by analyzing the highs and lows of the price. The first step in creating a trading strategy based on order block is to identify the market you want to trade. Take a gander at the general market structure (Record setting paces all around or Worse high points and Worse low points. Negative or Bullish). Market Design offers us inclination for exchanging chances. In the positively trending market, we generally hope to purchase

Dealers ought to then look for a break of the market structure. This could happen when the cost of the resource gets through a critical help or obstruction level, or when the cost frames another high or low that is beyond the ongoing business sector structure. Affirm the Break with Volume To affirm the break of market structure, brokers ought to likewise search for an expansion in exchanging volume. This can give extra affirmation that a change in market feeling is happening and improve the probability of a fruitful exchange.

Step 2: Identify Potential Order Blocks

Once the market structure has been broken, traders can then look for potential order blocks. Order Blocks are footprints left by the market when an impulsive move occurs. Order Block (OB) is the last inverse candle before serious areas of strength for the that makes an irregularity on the lookout. Whenever you have distinguished the market, the subsequent stage is to recognize key bullish or negative request block zones. These zones are regions where there is a huge lopsidedness among organic market. Search for a bullish or negative request block as per the higher time period pattern (Thus, on the off chance that the higher time span pattern is a downtrend, you would search for a negative order block and in the event that you are in a bullish market, you would bullish order block

Step 3: Enter or Exit Positions

Take a gander at the lower time periods and search for the lower time period affirmations. One request block has been recognized after the market structure break. Enter the exchange: When the request block level is affirmed, enter the exchange the bearing of the request block, putting in a stop-misfortune request at a proper level to restrict possible misfortunes in case of a market inversion. Deal with the exchange: When the exchange is open, screen it intently and be ready to change your stop-misfortune request and leave the exchange if vital. For extra affirmation can utilize the intersection factor any pointer

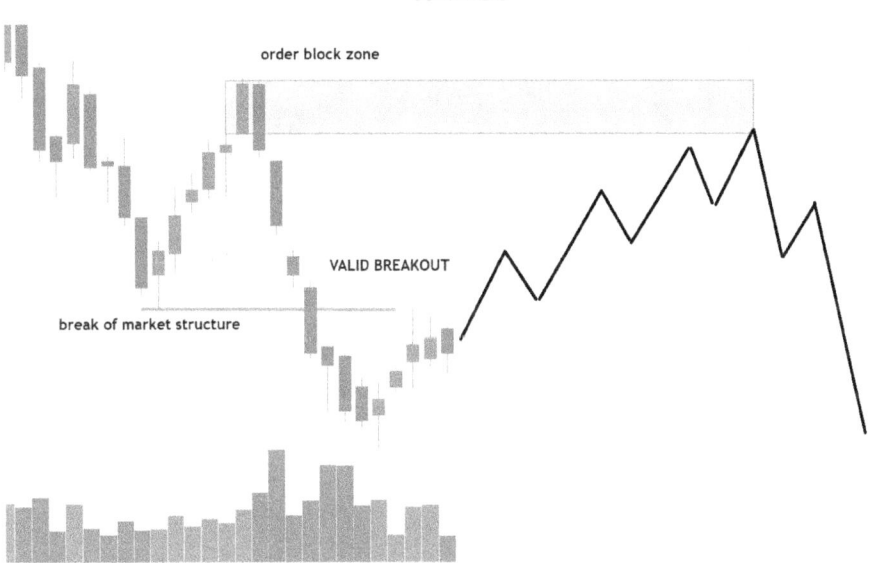

As you can see the market is in a downtrend making a lower low and lower high. Legitimate negative request obstructed shaped. Sit tight for any negative guard at the OB zone. OW actually look at underneath the refreshed outline.

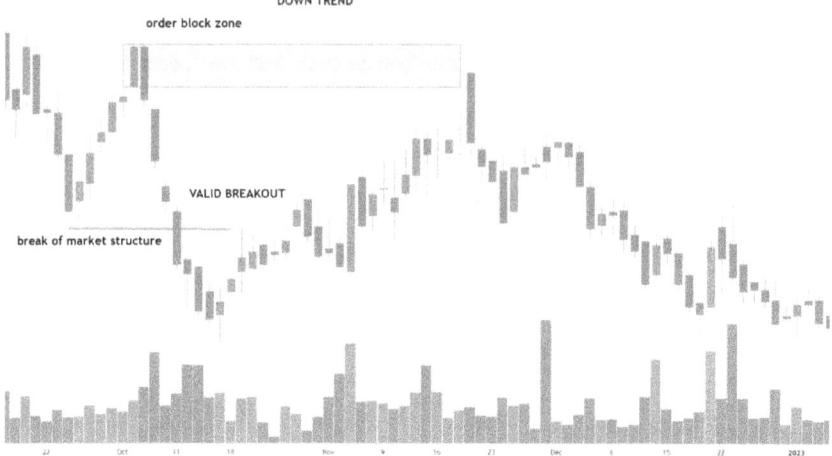

Here is another example

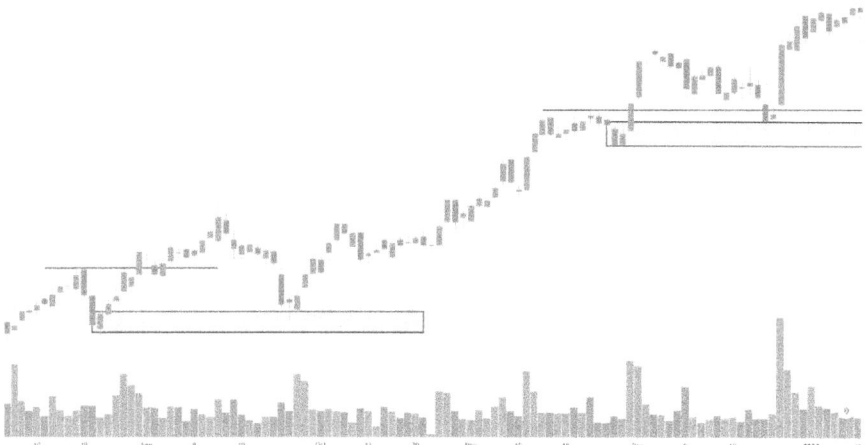

Here is another example

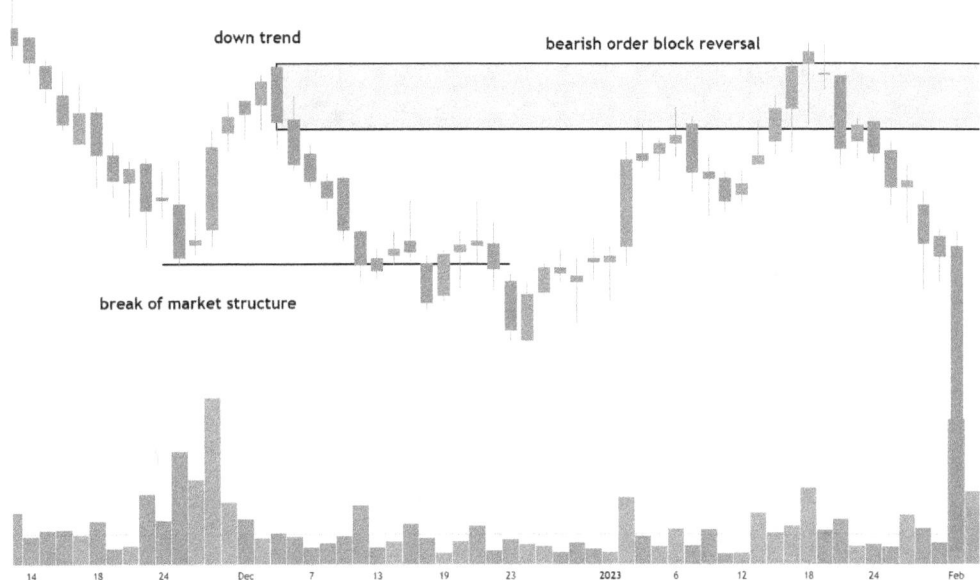

Change of Trend (Accumulation or Distribution)

It includes distinguishing key organic market zones on a value outline and sitting tight at a cost flip or change in the pattern to happen at those zones, which can flag a likely inversion. At the point when this design is broken, it can show a change in market opinion and give valuable open doors to merchants to enter or leave positions.

How Does Trend Change? From Bearish to Bullish

- Halting activity (halting the downtrend) or shortcoming in the pattern
- Change of conduct in range (strength of pattern changes from negative to bullish with regards to light and volume)
- Testing of supply (testing supply regardless of whether present)
- Break of market structure (assuming no stock found in testing activity)

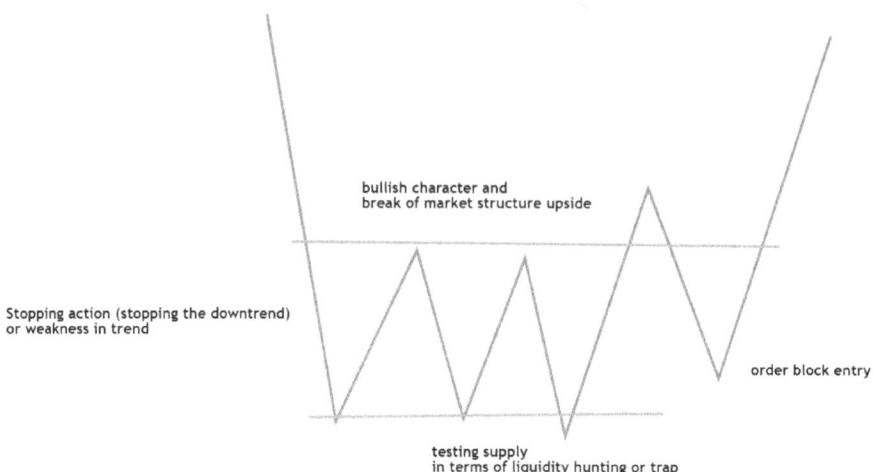

Now let's start all reversal market structures in detail.

Supply Demand Flip

- Cost made another high (market structure bullish interest in charge)
- It tried the last interest zone (OB zone) however the cost take a specialized skip from the interest zone rather than genuine purchasing, yet couldn't make a new higher high in the upturn.
- Rather than making a higher high in the upswing, it got through the last interest zone. Supply in charge leaving a stockpile zone behind
- At the point when the cost retests the stock zone we will sell.

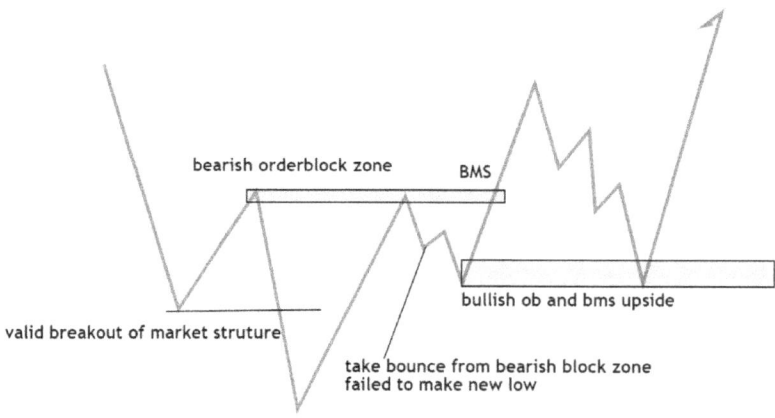

Step 1: Identify the Market Structure (and supply and demand zone)

- Recognize market interest zones: The initial step is to distinguish key organic market zones. Supply zones are regions where there is more selling tension than purchasing pressure, while request zones are regions where there is more purchasing strain than selling pressure.
- Trust that the cost will arrive at a stockpile or request zone: When market interest zones have been recognized, trust that the cost will arrive at one of these zones.

Also, sit tight for the flip of the zone

Search at a cost flip: When the cost arrives at a stock or request zone, search at a cost flip or change in the pattern to happen. This can be an inversion of the pattern, where an upturn changes to a downtrend or the other way around. Dealers ought to then look for a break in the market structure. This could happen when the cost of the resource gets through a critical help or obstruction level, or when the cost shapes another high or low that is beyond the ongoing business sector structure. Affirm the Break with Volume To affirm the break of market structure, dealers ought to likewise search for an expansion in exchanging volume. This can give extra affirmation that a change in market feeling is happening and improve the probability of a fruitful exchange.

Step 2: Identify Potential Order Blocks

Affirm the request block level: When the cost flip has happened, search for affirmation of the request block level by trusting that the cost will get back to the level and bob off. When the market structure has been broken, dealers can then search for potential request blocks. Request Blocks are effects had by the market when an imprudent move happens. Request Block (OB) is the last inverse flame before serious areas of strength for the that makes an unevenness on the lookout. Whenever you have recognized the market, the subsequent stage is to distinguish key bullish or negative request block zones. These zones are regions where there is a huge lopsidedness among organic market. Search for bullish or negative request blocks as per the higher time span pattern. Thus, on the off chance that the higher time period pattern is a downtrend, you would search for a negative request block and on the off chance that you are in a bullish market, you would bullish request block

Step 3: Enter or Exit Positions

Take a gander at the lower time periods and search for the lower time period affirmations. One request block has been distinguished after the market structure break. Enter the exchange: When the request block level is affirmed, enter the exchange the course of the request block, submitting a stop-misfortune request at a proper level to restrict expected misfortunes in case of a market inversion. Deal with the exchange: When the exchange is open, screen it intently and be ready to change your stop-misfortune request and leave the exchange if important. For extra affirmation can utilize the intersection factor as a marker.

1. Enter the Exchange: When the request block level is affirmed, enter the exchange the course of the cost flip, putting in a stop-misfortune request at a fitting level to restrict possible misfortunes in case of a market inversion.
2. Deal with the Exchange: When the exchange is open, screen it intently and be ready to change your stop-misfortune request and leave the exchange if fundamental.

Change of Character

BOF/TRAP. They face solid stockpile, then, at that point, the cost broke the untested lower time span request zone rather than skip or inversion, and each close to second request zone

AR BMS (STRNG SUPPLY IN Upswing) Supply in charge leaving a stock zone behind

Trial OF OB. At the point when the cost retests the stockpile zone we will sell.

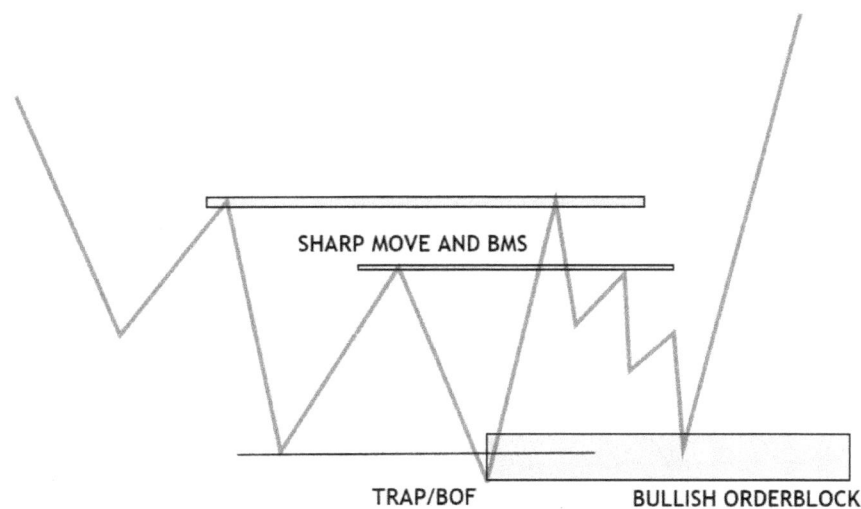

This example structure close to a higher time span supply/request zone .as the name proposes it includes shifts in market feeling and energy by searching for changes in the construction of cost activity on a cost graph

3. Distinguish untested higher time span supply/request zone and notice the cost activity around those levels. Search for indications of progress in the person or conduct of the cost activity, like the change in the course of the pattern

4. Distinguish potential request blocks: Request blocks are regions where enormous institutional dealers might have submitted trade requests, prompting critical cost developments.

5. Affirm the request block level: When an adjustment of character is noticed, affirm the request block level by trusting that the cost will get back to the level and skip off it or unite around it.

6. Enter the exchange: When the request block level is affirmed, enter the exchange the bearing of the adjustment of character, submitting a stop-misfortune request at a fitting level to restrict likely misfortunes in case of a market inversion.

7. Deal with the exchange: When the exchange is open, screen it intently and be ready to change your stop-misfortune request and leave the exchange if fundamental.

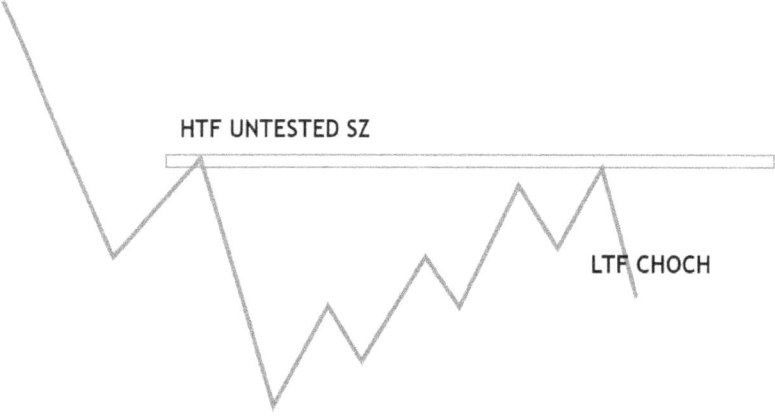

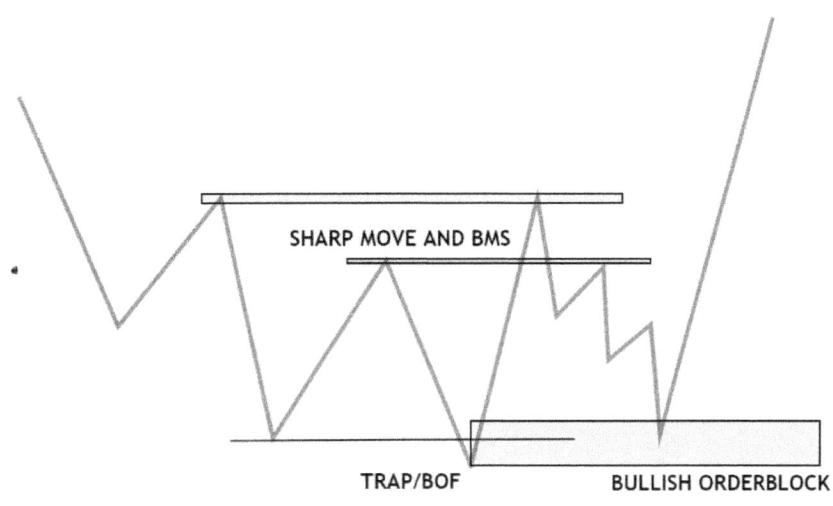

CHAPTER FOUR

WHAT IS SMC (Smart Money Concepts) Forex Strategy

What is SMC Forex

The least demanding strategy for portraying Adroit Money Thoughts trading is to say that it is cost action by a substitute name.

SMC consolidates utilizing commendable Forex considerations like normal market, regard models, and sponsorship and security from exchange, yet that all that has been given new names and portrayed another way.

SMC middle people recommend examination like "liquidity snatches" and "control blocks." While their expressing could sound new, when you look at SMC, you will remember it is a more standard exchanging approach than it appears from the beginning.

Might we at any point move something obtuse. Nothing awful can really be said about anybody utilizing SMC tolerating it works for them. Considering everything, we will be serious of explicit bits of SMC here, so be prepared for that.

SMC hypothesis

SMC isn't simply a Forex exchanging strategy, yet a whole viewpoint about how the business regions work.

From an overall perspective, SMC states that market creators (i.e., banks, versatile theories, and so on) are manipulative substances, and that besides, they are effectively prompting huge issues for retail transporters.

As shown by SMC, as a retail trained professional, you ought to collect your technique in regards to what's going on with the "wonderful cash" (i.e., the cash having a spot with market producers).

Without a doubt, you ought to try to design your compromising of how these market producers are exchanging. They are worried about supply, requesting, and market structure. Hence, as a SMC buyers, that is similarly the very thing that you are seeing while simultaneously going with your own exchange choices.

Where did SMC Forex trading come from

Clever Cash Considerations began with The Inside Circle Merchant (ICT), which is a program presented by a seller named Michael J. Huddleston. ICT offers several free assets as well as paid Forex tutor transport.

SMC focus thoughts and expressing

SMC sounds amazingly specific when you at initially begin investigating it. You could end up scratching your head at the critical language. To manage you, here are clarifications of several normal terms utilized by SMC shippers:

- Request disappoints: This expressing is utilized to investigate market income. Some SMC sellers say that sales blocks are a more "refined' thought than standard regular market, yet others challenge this case.
- Breaker blocks and equilibrium disappoints: These terms suggest help and prevention.
- Fair worth openings: This term proposes an imbalance. There are many kinds of openings, and they were totally perceived a shockingly lengthy time span back. Two or three models are standard openings, weariness openings, breakaway openings, and runaway openings.

You will find that other SMC considerations besides are ordinary to you once you sort out what the extravagant communicating is insinuating.

While dissecting the business regions, SMC zeros in a remarkable plan on "break of advancement" looking out, or "BOS."

Here is a chart showing breaks of improvement. Each time cost beats the past high, there is break of advancement. We then, at that point, see a differentiation in character (ChoCH) as cost drops down past actually settled lows.

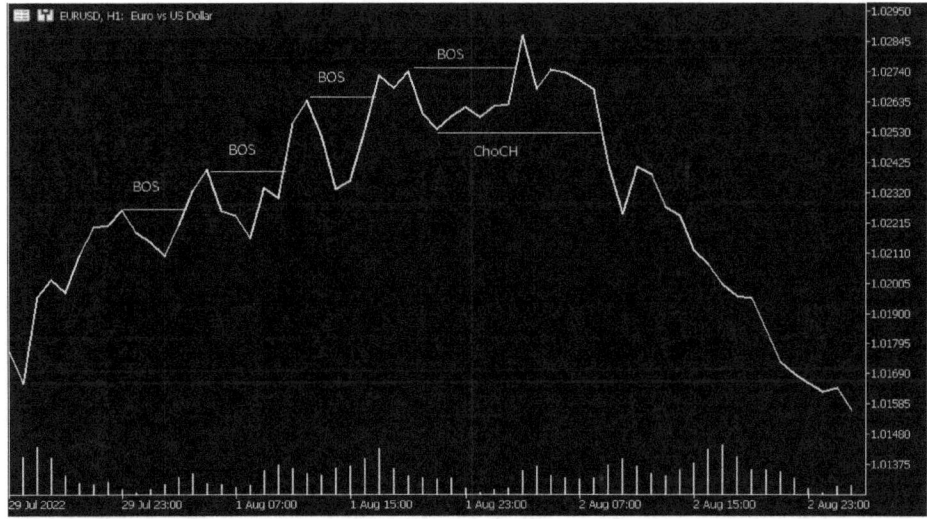

Conflicts about Splendid Money Thoughts in Forex trading

SMC is problematic for a few key reasons:

- The hypothesis behind it is off-base.
- SMC isn't "exchanging like the banks."
- Disregarding the way that it can work, it isn't new.

The imperfections in the hypothesis

What is the flaw in the hypothesis behind SMC? It returns to what we alluded to before about market creators.

SMC sellers say that controls by "savvy cash" entertainers are the clarification unequivocal SMC plans are illustrating. In any case, SMC gives no proof that these controls are happening or are liable for the models.

There is minimal thinking in announcing that unbelievable cash controls are making the models. The real factors confirm that banks and other enormous players move the business regions. Regardless, it isn't dependable with say that these

market not set in stone to get retail merchants and are effectively envisioning to control the business regions. Considering everything, their work in the business regions is to make liquidity.

In a general sense, market creators can't marshal the energy to think often about your reality. Retail transporters are fundamentally not that essential toward the day's end, when you gather them overall into a single unit. Does this mean market control is totally a legend? No. It winds up really working, yet not in the way that SMC depicts.

Equivalent to standard retail trading

SMC intermediaries acknowledge that they are exchanging like the market producers as opposed to exchanging like other retail sellers, and that this gives them an edge that their kindred retail vendors need.
In truth, SMC experts are exchanging precisely like their kindred retail buyers. They are not exchanging "like the banks."

New terms, old thoughts

At long last, the repackaging and rich stating is every one of the a wellspring of disrupting impact for a ton of middle people.
ICT has brought in gigantic measures of cash off of showing dealers SMC. Nothing horrible can really be said about that on a very basic level, since they are instructing frameworks that can be helpful. Nonetheless, two or three merchants feel that introducing
these old contemplation like they are spic and span is narcissistic here and there or another.
To add to that, understanding those new terms adds a degree of pointless disorder to the whole thing.
SMC doesn't precisely wait around as it in a general sense rebrand the wheel, placing it in another gathering. It is as of now a wheel. It turns in conclusively a comparative manner and can get you to precisely a comparative objective. Why go to the difficulty to secure capacity with another dialect to talk about something with which you right now are likely typical?
Taking everything into account (not all) merchants, it is going to be more clear to inspect backing and obstruction.

Potential gains and disadvantages of SMC

Experts of SMC:

- smart money contemplation exchanging accomplishes appear to work for explicit merchants. Expecting that it works for you, there is absolutely not a remarkable explanation not to utilize it. Having the decision to reliably get a handle on the thing cost is doing and benefit as its would like of acting is a more serious need than understanding the inspiration driving why cost is moving the status quo.
- Cost activity has a decades-in length history of making results for the
- larger part individuals across cash related standards, yet different resources also. Since SMC is repackaged cost development, it has out center.
- Certain individuals find cost activity all the more clear when it is introduced as SMC.
- While the hypothesis that massive affiliations are focusing in on retail experts is risky, it appears, apparently, to be feasible to recommend that more prominent foundations may a part of the time seek after extra unpretentious ones, conveying some of how the situation is turning out. Liquidity gets do exist, whether SMC is introducing them in an unrefined development. Along these lines, a piece of the hypothesis parts of SMC might be judicious, only not as SMC depicts them

Cons of SMC:

- A piece of the hypothesis parts of SMC don't seem to take a gander at when you consider how irrelevant retail facilitates are to the huge players. Enduring genuinely in all that SMC presents could accomplish disarray market basics.One can neither show nor nullify the speculations behind SMC. They are absolutely speculative, and just an insider would have the decision to make critical proof in one or the other heading. That deduces that nobody can insist that SMC's model of right, however it's unrealistic

- for anybody to 100 percent shame it then again. Nothing stays at this point with the exception of to battle thinking about how they trust concerning what affiliations answer.
- Changing around all the stating how SMC compartments make for an illogically tangled informational experience for cost activity, particularly expecting that you as of now are have some knowledge of the standard language of cost development. It could additionally make it harder for you to share what
- recognize with other people who talk the standard cost development language.
- A various group are switched off by the elitist persona integrating SMC, and feel it is manipulative to sell old contemplations like they are new. Besides, we are utilizing "sell" here according to a real viewpoint. While there are a ton of free SMC assets, you will run into a lot of pay entryways while trying to learn SMC.

Could it be prudent for you to trade using SMC

Stunning Cash Considerations exchanging would likely not be at any rate remarkable as it might be at the present time in the event that two or three transporters didn't envision that it is standard.

In the event that you truly like how SMC grants its stating and methodologies, absolutely, feel free to check it out.

Simply understand that the strategy is a repackaged kind of standard cost activity exchanging, and that you are doing besides as different other retail sellers.

Regardless, nothing horrible can be said about that, since standard cost development exchanging is a dependable method that has been valuable for specific sellers for a genuinely delayed time interval.

Tolerating the unusual communicating of SMC dumbfounds you or you are searching for extra free assets (there are paywalls for by a long shot most SMC programs), basically center around cost development. Regardless, will become familiar with exactly the same thing

www.ingramcontent.com/pod-product-compliance
Lightning Source LLC
Chambersburg PA
CBHW072239230526
45466CB00025B/2117